A Celebration of Summer

DAVID ADAM

'A man who has lost his sense of wonder is a man dead.'
William of Thierry (1085–1148)

Published in Great Britain in 2006

Society for Promoting Christian Knowledge
36 Causton Street
London SW1P 4ST

British Library Cataloguing-in-Publication Data
A catalogue record for this book is available from the British Library.

ISBN-13: 978–0–281–05714–6
ISBN-10: 0–281–05714–1

1 3 5 7 9 10 8 6 4 2

Designed and typeset by Monica Capoferri
Printed in Belgium

INTRODUCTION

Summer is when the annuals in our gardens come into full bloom: the results of our earlier labours are now seen. This is the time of the year to rejoice in what we have achieved through our dedication and planning, to give thanks for our own growth and abilities. Summer brings the opportunity to celebrate being part of this wonderful world and of what is going on around us. This is the time when the sun reaches its zenith, a time for us to enjoy the fullness of life, the high noon of our being. Now is the time of long days and brightness when we can extend ourselves, reach beyond our normal horizons and attempt new ventures. These are not days to shut ourselves in but rather to explore more of the world about us. Summer invites us to live more openly, to come out of doors and meet others to enjoy living.

The long hot days brings with them 'siesta time', the invitation to relax and let go, to lie back and feel the sunshine. We are invited to strip off layers of clothing and to allow the sun to touch us: we are able to be less formal in our dressing and in our eating. This is the time for picnics and barbecues. We should be able to have a break from our routine: to unwind for a while and alter our pattern of living. It is the time to walk along the shore at the water's edge and, if brave enough, to plunge into the deep.

We do not have to justify our enjoyment of the sunshine, it is offered freely for our delight. Let us luxuriate in the warmth of the day and the warmth of those who love us.

Summer should be the season when we least need to struggle. Although it has its own demands, it allows us time to get life into focus. This is the time to 'stop and stare': to be aware of the wonder of life and of all of creation; to open our eyes to the marvel of our own being. It is when we cease to live in wonder and awe that we begin to die. It is good to be able to say with Jacob (after his astounding dream of a ladder reaching into heaven): 'How awesome is this place!'

To bow before the mysteries that are all about us is to refocus on the depth of the world in which we live. The great division between peoples is not about ideologies but about sensitivity or the lack of it. When people are desensitized, they become dangerous to all about them. To be sensitive means to be aware of the other and the otherness of our world: to be focused on more than oneself. It means to become alive to the 'presence' which is with us and yet ever beyond us in its otherness. Once we are truly aware of the 'other', the whole world becomes holy ground, calling for love and adoration.

Come and celebrate summer and celebrate life.

I DANCED WITH THE SUN

I danced with the sun at dawn
As it rose and painted the sea
I danced with it in my heart
As merry as merry can be

I danced with the sun in the morning
As it drank the dew from the grass
I smelt the scent of new mown hay
And thought of a bonny lass

I danced with the sun at noon
In the brightness and heat of the day
Through woods and forests I danced
Without once losing my way

I danced with the sun in the evening
With a shimmer it trembled the air
I danced full of joy and serenity
In a world stressed with trouble and care

I danced with the sun in its setting
As it touched each cloud going down
I stood for a moment in silence
Then turned to the lights of the town

On 24 June, the day St John the Baptist's birth is commemorated, it used to be a tradition to dance around the 'St John's fire', to celebrate the sun's reaching its height at the summer solstice.

A BOUNDARY STONE

John, leaping in the womb
Kicking out at Elizabeth
To praise the coming Lord
Born to the priest Zechariah
And destined to be a prophet
The greatest of all the prophets
You stand as a boundary stone
Between the old and the new
Representative of the past
And herald, voice of the future
This your day, height of summer
But a greater light is to come
From one born in the darkest day
Now the tide will slowly turn
You will decrease with the day
The light will begin to fade
Until the carpenter's son is born
Then the light will increase
Bringing in the light of eternal day

The birth of St John the Baptist is celebrated on 24 June, close to the summer solstice and the longest day. From then on, the days start getting shorter and light decreases. The birth of Jesus is celebrated on 25 December, close to the winter solstice and the shortest day. From then on, the days get longer and the light increases.

THE CAR'S HANDEL

The engine ground to a halt
Its life was suddenly dead
There was no going on
I drifted into a lay-by
Off the main road of life
Joining the debris and weeds
Here people had dumped things
The unwanted lay around me
It was all depressing and dull
The bright spark of life gone
Stuck here, with my motor refusing to turn
I called for help
The day was bleak and grey
The sun had disappeared
Yet I was not totally alone
The car radio was still working
And the roadside repair man
Was now speeding on his way
I saw branches in full blossom
The sun broke through the cloud
'I know that my Redeemer liveth'
I heard played clear and loud

THE JOY OF WONDER

How mysterious the world is and how great a wonder is revealed in the smallest thing: in a flower, a leaf, a drop of water, in the atom. Nothing in this world is common or ordinary: all tremble with power and light; all are more insubstantial than we have ever dreamt of. Those who close their eyes and their hearts through cares or carelessness miss the joy and adventure that each event or thing offers. To find life dull, boring or empty shows we have not looked long enough or deeply enough at what is around us. Stay there long enough and mystery will rise before us. The world teems with wonder and excitement, if we will give it our attention and time. There is no thing or person that is not worthy of wonder and awe, of our time and attention.

Give your attention to anything and it will grow before you; it will become a subject in its own right, unfolding its own unique being.

If you are not moved by the world about you, feel your pulse and check your heart. You may have allowed something precious within you to die.

MIDSUMMER

Elder-bush stars shine
In a sun heavy sky
Sirocco scents
Sweep sheep-shorn fields

Hawthorn, pregnant green
Awaits the red of autumn
In gently swelling love
From sun, soil and rain

Swallows scythe the air
Harvesting the fiery sky
Pheasants laugh, curlew cry
No explanation or telling why

Sun sets in northern bound
Soon it will turn around
This is the moment to rejoice
To join with creation's voice

STAINED-GLASS PETER

You can see through the saints
Or let them colour your world
You can look past them
Or allow them to let the light in

Peter, made up of a glass mosaic
Holds the keys of heaven and earth
Can such a fragile human creature
Unlock the door to eternity?

Behind Peter the waves are fixed
Frozen breakers unable to overwhelm
Set in blue glass of wind and storm
The Christ stands shielding him from harm

Can this Peter add colour to my life
As the light dances on my skin?
I pray that here my storms may cease
And I will find new peace within

St Peter's Day is on 29 June.

TOUCHING BASE

I was wandering without watching
Not seeking any special place
When it appeared around a corner
Had I been here some time before?
What was it that spoke to me
That made me and the air tremble
That blazed out and bound me?
Something, Some One touching a nerve
Stringing my emotions with delight
Putting a joyful song in my heart
I am held as if by a strong magnet
I am caught in a radiance of light
Time is no longer. I have arrived
Full of awe, I am still for a while
Words cannot capture the moment
Yet I am afraid, and struggle to move on

AN ACT OF FAITH

I watched him as he talked excitedly at the breakfast table. Today, he was going to climb a mountain. He would rise to great heights and be much nearer the sun than we were! He knew that a bit of the ascent would be difficult, as there was a rock face to be climbed and there a great drop: 'It would be a long way to fall.' His eyes gleamed with expectation as he said: 'I know I will reach the top.' Someone asked him if he was afraid. 'No, not really,' was his reply. 'I have all the proper things to wear and to protect me on the mountain.' I do not think he had yet reached the age of eleven. How wonderful to be able to extend himself so easily and to face his day without fear.

Later, I saw him as he set out. He carried his own gear. He said to me, as he showed me his rope: 'Look at this strong rope. It will keep me fastened to my father. He has climbed many mountains and this is the first time he has let me go with him. If I slip, he will hold me and, when the way is hard, he will help me.' Then off he went with a bounce in his step on his great adventure.

It left me thinking how much I would like to venture with him. Often we dare not be adventurous because we are alone. We have cut ourselves free from our Father who is ever ready to help. We have broken our ties with our God and so dare not risk facing the mountain. Often we find ourselves facing great 'cliffs of fall' and without help.

As the little lad moved off, I made a promise: I would again bind myself to the Father, Son and Holy Spirit. That is what faith is – tying ourselves in trust and love to our God, knowing he will not let us fall and that, when we stumble, he will uphold us.

And how are we bound to God? We are bound with cords of love.

CORDS OF LOVE

I bind around myself today
The love of God the Father
Revealed through his creation

I bind around myself today
The love of Christ
And his offer of salvation

I bind around myself today
The love of the Spirit
Guiding and giving me inspiration

I bind around myself today
The love of the Holy Three
rejoicing in the presence of the Trinity

BEACH BEHAVIOUR

The combination of sun and sea has a liberating effect on most humans. In the summer months, the beach helps us to express the joy of being and the pleasure of the moment we are in. This begins with discarding our usual clothing for something brighter and often more revealing: more of our flesh is exposed to the sun and the salt air. There is a feeling of freedom and of levity, that it is good to be here.

Families live for the moment building sand castles. People of all ages are involved in projects that will last only until the tide comes in. There is little competition and a lot of cooperation. Fathers often feel a greater need than their children to dig moats and create turrets. And for all, it is a precious moment when the sea fills the ditch to the moat.

Life is an exploration with rocks and caves to visit, to see what mysteries lie there. The thrill at finding a crab or a sea anemone is shared by all the adventurers. It is a time for collecting shells and avoiding jellyfish: sometimes the discovery of a shell is like finding treasure and it will be taken home as a memento.

Lovers draw hearts with arrows and write their names in the sand. Some utter a prayer that their relationship may last a tide change as they walk, arm in arm, along the shoreline. Bathers brave the cold of the sea, unafraid of the deep. Others dressed in their wetsuit armour, like knights of the deep, ride the waves. Most are content to paddle at the edge and jump each wave.

It is time for rest and relaxation. Deckchairs, windbreaks, towels and little tents brighten the shore. Resting in a deckchair, doing nothing, soaking up the sun, idly watching the kites dipping in the gentle breeze – none of these requires any explanation. Life is here to be enjoyed and needs no justification.

TRT

Trt, trt
There is no word
For the sound of the pine cone
As it opens its heart to the sun
Seed releasing
Life increasing
Before its work is done
Trt, trt
There is no word for the pine sound
It is different with every one

Amo, amas, amat
There is no word for love
Though we have invented many a one
Life enriching
World transforming
Its work is never done
Amo, amas, amat
There is no word for love
For it is different for everyone

THE MAGDALENE

Mary
Loose as your lovely hair
Tempting men and angels
Living life for the moment
Appearing to be adventuring
Yet a captive to your past
Held by history and demons
I feel your tears as they fall
I am aware of your heartbreak
Your spirit struggling and bound
Mary, today, you are set free
Free to let the tears touch me
To pour out your heart to me
To touch my feet with your hair
The past is gone for ever, forgiven
Mary
You are loving and loved
And we all need your warm heart

St Mary Magdalene's Day is on 22 July.

SUMMER SILENCE

'Stop and seek the silence,' she said
I could die or drown in its depths
'Enter into the stillness of your mind'
Dangerous dragons dwell in the deep
'Empty out the wandering thoughts'
I would be drained or dredge up sludge
'Launch out into the deep'
Now, I had heard those words before
This was a call to adventure
I plunged in, as asked, heart first
Great waves of fear broke over me
For a brief moment, I floundered
Suddenly I was raised upwards
Into the light and love of the Lord
Into the stillness and sunshine of summer

LAMMAS PRAYER

God, through your grace and goodness
We are guests at your table
And we have this bread to set before you

With this bread, we offer the wonders of our world
The sun and rain, the soil and the air
The whole beauty and balance of creation

With this bread, we give thanks for living things
For flower, fruit and field, the richness of the harvest
For the fish of the sea and the birds that fly

With this bread, we bring before you our labours
The work of farmer, miller, baker and shopkeeper
All that we strive for and seek to achieve

With this bread, we offer you our prayers
For all who are growing in wisdom and in stature
For all schools, colleges and universities

We have this bread to set before you
Which the earth has given, human hands have made
It will become for us the Bread of Life

Blessed be God for ever!

Lammas Day is on 1 August. The word 'Lammas' first appears in the writings of King Alfred and is derived from the words 'loaf' and 'mass'. In the early English Church, it was traditional to consecrate a loaf made from the first ripened corn on this day. Lammas Day was thus an early Harvest Festival and may have been inspired by the Hebrew Feast of Weeks, when a sheaf of the first barley harvest was offered (see Leviticus 23.15–21).

INVITATION TO A HOLY DAY

Come be a pilgrim, walk on the sand
That glorious mixture of sea and land
Here the light is twice as bright
Can our eyes cope with the sight?
Let our hearts lift on the shore
Which is the edge of the evermore
As we absorb the sky, feel the earth
May they bring us to new birth
Soon the tide will remove every trace
Of life's troubled and hectic pace
As we relax our bodies, let go all strain
We'll find the strength to start again
Leaving behind our daily routine
To return restored, fresh and clean
Let us enjoy this holy place
Rest awhile in God's love and grace

It is good to place ourselves on the borderlands and know that we belong to two places. We all belong to the world of matter and the world of the spirit, and it is of vital importance that we enjoy both.

PRESSED FLOWERS

Pressed flowers are like words
Longing for an experience lost
Seeking to retain what has been
Unable to be captured between pages
We can still see and touch them
But where is the coolness of the stem
And the heavenly scent of summer
The joy of them dancing in the breeze?

Words cannot capture experience
Life will not be pressed into pages
Words cannot hold the Almighty Word
God made flesh and living among us
Pressed flowers are like words
Living flowers are an experience

JUST DRIFTING

After pulling on oars and going against the current, it is good to drift. There is a great enjoyment in testing oneself against a strong current, in using one's whole body and mind in the struggle to achieve. We all need aims and objectives; we need to decide where we are going; but we also need to know when we have arrived and we can relax. There is something wonderful about being borne along by the river or resting in the centre of a lake. There is a special moment when we can ship our oars and take a more leisurely pace. It is good to know we can dip our hands into the cool water and enjoy all that is around us.

The element that we were battling against has become our friend. Too often we spend our whole lives going against the current or cutting across the grain. There is something marvellous, blessed, about being able to let go. So often, the thing we wrestle with seeks to be our friend. It is a joy not to have to do anything except correct our journey a little every now and then: a gentle tug on the rope or touch of the rudder.

One of the arts of living is to know when to go with the stream and drift: to relax all our muscles, to lie back and enjoy being carried. Very often this relief comes as a result of our efforts and we should recognize this. Every day we need to learn to drift for a time, to stop in the stream and trail our fingers in the sparkling waters. We can do this in the city with music or a good play. Great halls and cathedrals are wonderful places to let the music drift around us and to carry us. At home, we can get the same experience from a good book or just by sitting back for a while. It is amazing how energy is renewed and the spirit uplifted when we learn just to drift for a spell.

TRANSFIGURATION

Brighter than the brightest sun
Radiant is his transfigured face
Giving light to a darkened world
Promising life and love eternal
An explosion of love from the cloud
With a power beyond belief
Giving us a glimpse of glory

We abused our God given power
To destroy, distort and disfigure
For a moment bright as the sun
Then the mushroom cloud of darkness
Radiating death and destruction
Leaving us spiritually unprepared
For the age of exploding atoms

Feast of the Transfiguration of Jesus is on 6 August – the day the atomic bomb was dropped on Hiroshima in 1945.

UNDER THE ANAESTHETIC

The street is a surreal cemetery
Shimmering in the summer heat
Bare bones walking without spirit
Life-drained bodies on autopilot
Drifting in a perpetual dream
Going nowhere, yet forever travelling
Wrapt in ephemeral goods
Doing nothing of any consequence
The mind is out of gear
And the soul is departed

THE VIBRANT PRESENCE

Space is not empty
There is a presence
Vibrant between the stars
Unmeasurable
Incomprehensible
As silent as light
A brooding, loving being
There again between the atoms
Dancing in the spaces
Watching
Waiting for us
To come and join the dance
Nothing is without mystery
Calling for wonder and awe
The Presence prevails
Pervades all there is

WANDERING IN WONDER

Life is always wonderfully awesome
Our minds made for marvel and miracle
Spirits soar with secret and surprise
To be awake is to see the strangeness
Of the other coming in many disguises
To be told of pulsars and black holes
And dream of radiance and darkness
To hear of our own genetic make-up
The DNA spiral and the mystery of life
Is to realize we hardly know our selves
Looking at microscopic patterns
We see more space than solidity
Every creature carries a universe within
We have seen and we have heard
But we have hardly understood
There is much beyond the frontiers
Of the mind as we face the other
The journey towards another
Is wonderfully awesome and eternal

ILLUSTRATIONS

A Summer Day (oil on board) by Charles David Jones Bryant (1883–1937), Private Collection, © Whitford Fine Art, London, UK/Bridgeman Art Library. The publisher has been unable to trace the copyright holder and would be grateful to receive any information as to their identity and whereabouts.

Boulogne Sands by Sir Walter Russell (1871–1903), © The Potteries Museum and Art Gallery, Stoke-on-Trent, UK/Bridgeman Art Library.

Saint John the Baptist by Michelangelo Merisi da Caravaggio (1573–1610), Nelson Gallery, Kansas City, USA, © Photo Scala, Florence.

Summer Blossom in Battersea Park (oil on canvas) by Philip Sutton (b. 1928), © Phillip Sutton 2006. All Rights Reserved, DACS. Private Collection/Bridgeman Art Library.

Portrait of Taylor and McKenzie (oil on canvas) by James Hill (1930–2004), The Sullivan Collection/Bridgeman Art Library.

The Swineherd, Brittany, 1888 (oil on canvas) by Paul Gauguin (1848–1903), Norton Simon Foundation, San Marino, California, USA/ www.superstock.co.uk.

St Peter, design by Ford Madox Brown from a stained glass window by the William Morris Company in Jesus Church, Troutbeck, Cumbria, UK, www.stainedglassphotography.com.

The Church at Auvers-sur-Oise, 1890 (oil on canvas) by Vincent van Gogh (1853–90), Musée d'Orsay, Paris, France/Bridgeman Art Library.

Swaledale, Yorkshire (oil on canvas) by Josephine Trotter (b. 1940/British), www.superstock.co.uk.

Icon with the *Trinity* by Andrei Rublev (1360–c. 1430), Tretyakov State Gallery, Moscow, Russia, © Photo Scala, Florence.

View to Redend Point by Charles Neal (b. 1951/British), www.superstock.co.uk.

Afternoon at Pardigon by Henri Edmond Cross, Musée d'Orsay, Paris, France, © Photo Scala, Florence.

Mary Magdalene, 1877 (oil on canvas) by Dante Charles Gabriel Rossetti (1828–82), Delaware Art Museum, Wilmington, USA, Samuel and Mary R. Bancroft Memorial/Bridgeman Art Library.

Lighthouse at Two Lights, 1929 (oil on canvas) by Edward Hopper (1882–1967), Metropolitan Museum of Art, New York, USA/Bridgeman Art Library. The publisher has been unable to trace the copyright holder and would be grateful to receive any information as to their identity and whereabouts.

Still Life with Loaves of Bread (oil on canvas) by Ilya Ivanovich Mashkov (1881–1944), State Russian Museum, St Petersburg, Russia/ Bridgeman Art Library.

The Sea at Southwold, Hot June Day by Hugo Grenville (b. 1958), Private Collection/Bridgeman Art Library.

In the Garden (Celia Thaxter in her Garden), 1892 by Childe Hassam, Smithsonian American Art Museum, Washington DC, USA, © Photo Smithsonian American Art Museum/Art Resource/Scala, Florence.

Calm Morning, 1904 (oil on canvas) by Frank Weston Benson (1862–1951), Museum of Fine Arts, Boston, Massachusetts, USA, Gift of the Charles A. Coolidge Family/Bridgeman Art Library. The publisher has been unable to trace the copyright holder and would be grateful to receive any information as to their identity and whereabouts.

Transfiguration by Giovanni Battista Paggi (1554–1627), San Marco, Florence, Italy, © Photo Scala, Florence.

Sixth Avenue I, 1986 (oil on canvas) by Bill Jacklin (contemporary artist), Private Collection/Bridgeman Art Library.

Café Terrace, Place du Forum, Arles, 1888 (oil on canvas) by Vincent van Gogh (1853–90), Rijksmuseum Kroller-Muller, Otterlo, Netherlands /Bridgeman Art Library.

The Upper Thames at St John's Meadows Near Buscot, Oxfordshire, Gloucestershire, 2003 (oil on canvas) by Charles Neal (b. 1951/British), www.superstock.co.uk.